FORT WORTH LIBRARY

P9-DCF-957

CHILDREN 940.53 THOMSON
   2011
Thomson, Ruth
Terezin

Wedgwood   ✓ 03/13/2012

WEDGWOOD BRANCH

Terezín

VOICES FROM THE HOLOCAUST

RUTH THOMSON

CANDLEWICK PRESS

Copyright © 2011 by Franklin Watts

All rights reserved. No part of this book may
be reproduced, transmitted, or stored in an
information retrieval system in any form or by any
means, graphic, electronic, or mechanical, including
photocopying, taping, and recording, without
prior written permission from the publisher.

First U.S. edition 2011

Library of Congress Cataloging-in-Publication
Data is available.

Library of Congress Catalog Card Number pending

ISBN 978-0-7636-4963-0

SCP 15 14 13 12 11 10
10 9 8 7 6 5 4 3 2 1

Printed in Humen, Dongguan, China

This book was typeset in Gill Sans and Futura.

Candlewick Press
99 Dover Street
Somerville, Massachusetts 02144

visit us at www.candlewick.com

The author would like to thank the following for
their help in the preparation of this book: Eva
Nemcová, Iva Gaudesová, Martina Šiknerová, Jaroslava
Nytlová, and Dr. Jan Munk at Pamatnik Terezín;
Michal Frankl, Michaela Siderberg, Noemi Holeková,
and Martin Jelinek at the Jewish Museum in Prague;
the Sound Archives at the Imperial War Museum
in London; the Wiener Library in London; the
Holocaust Education Trust; Jacqueline Hall, Monica
Stoppleman, Pam Dix, Caroline Pick, and Su Kent.

Note: Some extracts in this book have been shortened
to make them suitable for the intended readership.

Contents

Terezín: Theresienstadt

Terezín is a small fortress town in the Czech Republic. It was built in 1780 by the Austrian emperor Joseph II and named after his mother, Maria Theresa. The town might forever have remained largely unknown to the rest of the world. Instead, it attained notoriety.

During the Second World War, the Nazis turned Terezín into a ghetto and renamed it Theresienstadt. Here, they imprisoned thousands of Jewish people—first Czechs, then Germans, and, later, Danish and Dutch. Many were then sent to their deaths at Auschwitz.

Piecing Together the Story

This book about what happened in Terezín has been compiled using the words of Jewish people who were transported there during the war. Some of the extracts come from secret diaries of inmates, both adults and children, who recorded their everyday lives, feelings, and observations. Although some of these people perished, their documents were found and published once the war was over.

Other extracts are taken from the written memoirs of survivors who wanted to tell their own moving stories for future generations. In the past twenty years or more, museums and other organizations have interviewed many survivors, recording their memories of life before, during, and after the war. Some extracts are taken from these personal testimonies, which are now available to the public.

▽ **The town square of Terezín today**
During the war, the building on the far left was a home for infants. Next to it, now shrouded in scaffolding, was a bank. To the right of the bank was a children's home, in a building that now houses the Terezín Ghetto Museum.

The Pictures

The words are complemented by compelling, and sometimes troubling, visual images made by inmates. Many of these pictures were hidden just before people were transported to death camps and only found again after the war. Some were made by children or amateur painters. Most were created by artists who were already accomplished professionals when they arrived at Theresienstadt.

The Nazis forced a number of these artists to work in one of two studios. Those in the technical drafting studio illustrated official reports, maps, and charts, while those in the art studio had to create paintings and decorations for Nazi homes and buildings. In their spare time, however, many of these artists drew secret, and very different, pictures, revealing the reality of life in the town.

1933–1938
Hitler and the Jews

In the early 1930s, Jews made huge contributions to the industrial, social, and artistic life in Germany. But Adolf Hitler, who became chancellor in 1933, blamed them for Germany's defeat in the First World War and its economic crisis. He was convinced that getting rid of Jews would help make Germany powerful again.

Dismissed and Banned

Once in power, Hitler and the Nazi party began passing laws against the Jews—expelling them from the army, dismissing them from the civil service, and banning them from practicing as doctors or lawyers. Soon Jews were banned from cinemas, theaters, sports, and social clubs. They were no longer allowed to go into cafés or parks. The Nazi-controlled media spread anti-Jewish propaganda promoting the idea of a superior Aryan "master race" of tall, blond, and blue-eyed Germans.

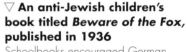

▽ **An anti-Jewish children's book titled *Beware of the Fox*, published in 1936**
Schoolbooks encouraged German children to be anti-Jewish. These caricatures contrast the Nazi Aryan ideal with a Jew.

Bullied and Beaten Up

    After 1933 it was just accepted that if you were a Jewish child, you were liable to be beaten up, bullied, or whatever else they wanted to do with you. It was no use appealing to the policemen or teachers because they're not supposed to interfere or even be interested in helping you because you are perceived as an enemy of the state.

John Silberman, a German schoolboy

Isolating the Jews

An onslaught of Nazi laws made Jews more and more isolated from the rest of the German population. In 1935, the Nuremberg Laws stripped Jews of their citizenship and prohibited Jews from marrying non-Jews. Soon, Jews were banned from having any professional jobs. By 1938, Jews had to have the letter *J* stamped on their passports and Jewish children were banned from state schools.

Kristallnacht

A turning point for the Jews came on the night of November 9, 1938, which became known as *Kristallnacht* (Night of Broken Glass). In well-organized riots, the Nazis burned synagogues and smashed Jewish shop windows all over Germany and Austria. Approximately 30,000 men were arrested and imprisoned in concentration camps.

▽ **The burned interior of a synagogue**
At least 1,000 synagogues were burned down or demolished during *Kristallnacht*.

The Burning of a Synagogue

" We received a telephone call from a very close friend of ours, who lived in the street opposite our synagogue, to say the synagogue was in flames and the SA (stormtroopers) wouldn't let the fire engine put out the fire, only making sure that it sprayed water on the adjoining houses. We were very anxious and worried and when I looked at the ceiling, this was quite red from the flames of the synagogue which was only in the next street. " Freddie Knoller, an Austrian schoolboy

Emigration

After *Kristallnacht,* Jews realized that it was no longer safe for them to live in Germany or Austria. Hundreds of thousands left for other European countries or for America.

It was a well-planned destruction of Jewish property. After that, things got very, very serious.

John Fink, a German schoolboy

The Germans Invade

Czechoslovakia was created in 1918. Twenty-two percent of its population was German, living in Sudetenland, an area lost by Germany after World War I. In 1938, as part of his plan to regain German lands, Hitler annexed Sudetenland. In 1939, he invaded the rest of Czechoslovakia and established the Protectorate of Bohemia and Moravia.

It was a small country under complete siege.

Hana Pravda, a young Czech actress

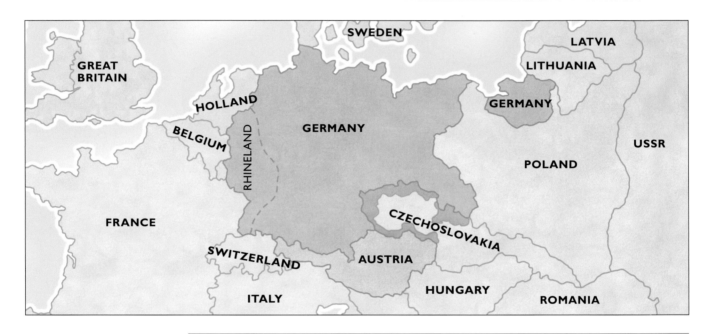

△ **Map of Europe**
This map shows Europe in 1939. Germany had already occupied the Rhineland and invaded Austria. Sudetenland is shaded in pink, distinct from the rest of Czechoslovakia.

The Day the Germans Invaded

" It was a Wednesday in March 1939, about six o'clock in the morning—we were three children and parents, a family of five. My father came to wake us up and he said, 'Quick, quick, children, come to the window. There are columns of German army motor-cyclists trundling through the town.'

Of course, a child is curious. We all rushed to the window and had a look. It looked very menacing. They were helmeted and *drrrr, drrrr,* one after another in long columns like black ants. And, of course, we didn't quite know what the consequences would be, but the feeling was very menacing. Then we listened to the radio, which had a feeling of urgency and they were repeating, 'Stand by. Stand by.' When we heard they'd reached Prague and occupied the castle and there was a big upheaval, we knew that was the beginning of the end. "

Zdenka Ehrlich, a young Czech woman

△ **Hitler's arrival**
Hitler drove through the town of Brno, in the southeast of the country, when the Germans took over Czechoslovakia.

How Life Changed for Czech Jews

    Most people stayed indoors when the Germans came, but there were some who welcomed them. These people hated the Jews, were envious of those who had more than they, and now it was their turn to show their meanness. The Germans took over quickly—some people were arrested on the first day. Soon orders appeared on bulletin boards and in newspapers. We Jews were hit the hardest. 'Jews not permitted' signs appeared in cinemas, the coffeehouses, streetcars, public buildings, etc. Schools were ordered not to allow us in; public swimming areas were prohibited to us. My friendship with non-Jewish boys came to an end. We were required to wear a yellow star of David on each outer garment, over the lapel. School became a private affair in the living room. Groups of kids met and were instructed by young Jewish teachers. Occasionally, a father of some of our friends would be arrested and he would disappear. We had to give away our car, and Father closed down his medical office. As time went on, we were ordered to give up half our apartment.

    A special relationship developed among the young, who were surrounded by the general community and vilified in the newspapers and on the radio. We now found new strength and helped each other. What would happen when our savings were gone and nothing would be left to live on was a big question mark.

John Freund, a Czech schoolboy

△ **The yellow star of David**
From September 1941, a law required Czech Jews to wear a yellow star with the word *Jude* (Jew) at its center, sewn onto their outer clothes. This marking was designed both to identify and to humiliate Jews.

GERMANY POLAND

Terezín
Eger R. Elbe R.

Prague Olomouc
Plzeň

Brno

AUSTRIA

△ **The position of Terezín**
Terezín is about 35 miles north of Prague on a grassy plain where two rivers, the Elbe and the Eger, meet.

▽ **The ramparts**
The star-shaped fortress town is encircled by two rings of high embankment walls, with a deep grassy moat between them.

1941 October
From Fortress to Ghetto

Life for Czech Jews became increasingly restricted. Then, in September 1941, Reinhard Heydrich, a prominent Nazi, became head of the protectorate. He held two top-secret meetings with other leading Nazis at his office in Prague. They decided to turn Terezín into a ghetto where they would imprison every Czech Jew.

Records from the Nazis' First Meeting on October 10, 1941

❝ Terezín might be most suitably used as a ghetto.... Transport to the ghetto of Terezín would not require much time. Two or three trains containing a thousand Jews each could be sent every day. According to the well-tried method, let each Jew take with him luggage up to 50 kilograms in weight and food for a fortnight up to four weeks, which will make it easier for us. Straw will be allocated to the empty flats in the ghetto, for beds would take up too much room. ❞

> Jews from Bohemia and Moravia will be assembled for evacuation. The Czechs there will be advised to move elsewhere. Fifty to sixty thousand Jews may be comfortably accommodated in Terezín. From there the Jews will go East. After the complete evacuation of the Jews, Terezín will, according to a perfect plan, be settled by Germans and become a center of German life. Under no account must any details of these plans become public.

The choice of Terezín

The Germans chose Terezín because it was not far from Prague and only a couple of miles from a convenient railway station. The town's intact fortifications, with high walls, a deep moat, and only a few entrances, made it easy to guard. The streets, laid out in a grid, were lined with 219 houses, as well as eleven huge soldiers' barracks, which could immediately house large numbers of people. The town also had storehouses, shops, schools, offices, a church, a town hall, a main square, and several parks. On the other side of the river was the Small Fortress, a former prison. Germans were already garrisoned there by 1941 and were using it as a prison for Czech political prisoners.

△ **Entrance to the cell blocks in the Small Fortress**
Arbeit macht frei is German for "Work will set you free." This slogan was placed above the entrance to several Nazi concentration camps, including Auschwitz.

△ **Watchtower**
This tower overlooks the execution cells and yard of the Small Fortress.

◁ **Bridge over the moat**
This is one of the original entrances to Terezín.

1941–1942
Deportations

In November 1941, two work crews of engineers, doctors, carpenters, and other craftsmen went to Terezín to get it ready to accommodate thousands of people. In December, 2,000 Jews were deported to the town from Prague. By September 1942, more than 50,000 people, the majority of all Czech Jews, had been deported to Terezín.

△ **Transport number**
Every transport had its own initials. Every deportee was given an individual number.

Getting Ready for a Transport

❝ We were called to a meeting, given a transport number, and told that on such a day we will have to leave the house. The numbers were S204, S205, and S206, for my mother, my brother, and my sister, and I got S216. Now came a big commotion because we didn't know where we were going. Nobody ever knew where they were going. Somebody came and said, 'It might last longer than you think. Perhaps you should have only winter things.' Somebody else said, 'Forget about winter things—put in soap, cigarettes.'

We all gathered at the local station, were transported to Plzeň, from which the complete transport was loaded into a train—it was a normal train—heading 'destination unknown.' ❞

Zdenka Ehrlich

There was one transport after the other. You knew you wouldn't get away anymore.

Jan Hartman, a Czech schoolboy

▽ **The walk to Theresienstadt**
It was a two-mile walk from the station to Theresienstadt.

The Day of the Transport

❝ When we arrived at the railway station, we were all standing there, everybody with the Jewish star and our two pieces of luggage, and they told us to get into the train. We arrived at Olomouc, the capital of Moravia, and that was our first humiliation and shock. It was early in the morning, four o'clock, and we were put in five rows, with the luggage, which was terribly heavy—my grandfather, my mother, and me. They took us to a big gym in a school. The Germans asked us to hand in all our documents, birth certificates and all, and to hand over the keys to our home. We were left with those two suitcases. My mother still had her engagement ring and her wedding ring. I had a little golden chain and a charm bracelet. Those little things were something to remember from the past. ❞

Edith Baneth, a Czech teenager

The Journey to Theresienstadt

"We must have traveled sixteen to twenty hours. Night had fallen again. The train slowed down, stopped, a few more jerks, and we arrived. Again the shouting: 'Raus, raus, everybody out. Take everything with you, line up by fours.' We are in a little two-track railway station with two sidings, a typical branch-line station: *Bohusovice-Bauschowitz* says the sign.

At last the doors of the freight cars are thrown open; fresh air replaces the unbearable body odor and the stench. Bleary-eyed figures, totally exhausted, deathly tired, unwashed, stumble out of the cars: frightened women, children; the men, cursing their fate but still hoping. All of them grab their rucksacks and their hand luggage and start to move forward. The SS escorts bark as usual and drive their 1,000 victims to move at a faster pace. The column falls into smaller groups. Despite all the yelling, the old people weighed down by their baggage simply cannot continue and collapse on the roadside. The frightened, starved children scream; the stronger people lumber forward under the weight of their luggage.

Ghetto Theresienstadt could not be seen at all from Bauschowitz. The only thing visible was an elongated green hill with a flat top and grass-covered slopes. The upper part of a church steeple rose abruptly out of the green belt, indicating that behind the green hill there had to be a town. The sloping hillsides were the fortification buildings."

Norbert Troller, a Czech architect

△ **The station sign**
The Germans renamed the Bohusovice railway station *Theresienstadt-Bauschowitz*.

We were not allowed to walk on the footpath. We had to walk in the road.

Lily Fischl, a young Czech woman

Arrival at Theresienstadt

When the first Czech Jews arrived, the town was scarcely habitable. There were not enough beds. Washing and lavatory facilities were short of water. Kitchens were not properly equipped. New arrivals were shocked.

Theresienstadt, a Ghetto?

❝ We thought we would get apartments there and would live, all Jewish people from the whole country, all concentrated in this one town and would live just a normal life, but in a ghetto. Ghettos had existed before Hitler, so we imagined it as a ghetto. ❞ **Edith Baneth**

Systematic Looting

The Nazis looted the homes that the Jews had left behind, stealing silver, china, furniture, pianos, books, and carpets. Some things were stored in synagogues, but the best were sold or shipped to Germany.

We thought Terezín was a ghetto.
Edith Baneth

▽ **A transport has arrived**
František M. Nagl
Inmates left their luggage in the courtyard of a barracks before going to register their arrival.

Registration and Robbery

New arrivals had to leave their luggage in a pile and go to a center nicknamed the *Schleuse* (sluice) by inmates. There, they filled in registration forms and received food, bath, and laundry vouchers. All their valuables were confiscated. Everyone was quizzed about their work skills and given a medical examination before being deloused at a separate delousing station.

The Nazis meanwhile raided everyone's suitcases for money, jewelry, cigarettes, soap, and other precious articles, leaving people only essential clothes and bed linen. They stole whatever they wanted for themselves, sent the best clothes and shoes to people in bombed German cities, and stored the rest of the things in warehouses. Some of these were later sold back to the inmates in the ghetto shops.

The new inmates spent several nights crowded together before being allocated housing.

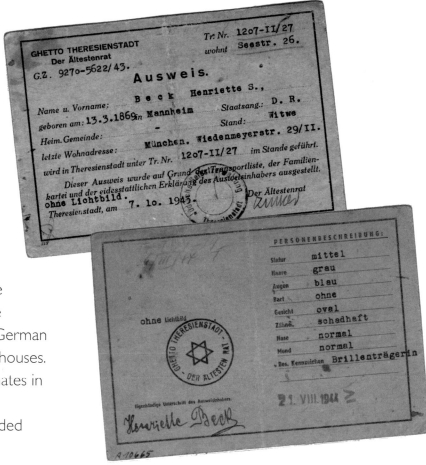

△ **An identity card (front and back)**
Everyone was issued an identity card. The front showed the person's name, date of birth, and last address. The back listed identifying features, such as hair and eye color.

The First Few Nights

66 They put us in Magdeburg Barracks. We lay on the floor, one next to the other. We just had little sack and straw-filled mattresses, our suitcases next to us—children, men, and women all together. There were some latrines that the soldiers used to use and washing facilities where the soldiers used to wash. That was just for a few days. Then they separated the men, women, and children into different places. 99 **Edith Baneth**

66 During the night we were transferred to a barracks. We were led up to the loft in one of these barracks and had the shock of our lives. We were provided with one straw mattress each and a very thin blanket and that was all. The first night was a real nightmare. I got maybe a hundred fleabites and there were lots of lice as well. So within a few days I was simply full of these big bites and I was told not to scratch because they could become very easily infected. 99
Aron Sloma, a Danish inmate

Terezín was a town of pretense.

Bedrich Lederer, a German artist

△ **Portrait of Bedrich Fritta**
Leo Haas

▽ **The Drafting Room
of the Technical Office**
Leo Haas
Working here gave artists access to
scarce drawing materials, which they
used for their own secret work.

Artist Witnesses

Among the first arrivals was Bedrich Fritta. A successful graphic artist, he was put in charge of the technical drawing studio. Here, a group of professional artists made architectural drawings and illustrated official reports and charts for the Nazis. In their free time, they made secret drawings, documenting overcrowding and suffering in the ghetto.

How Artists Created Their Pictures in Secret

❝ Naturally, we were soon making use of this activity, that was sanctioned by the SS and which we exercised as part of our work, to make studies and sketches of life within the ghetto, camouflaged as official work. Especially Fritta and I were constantly encouraged to create this unique documentary testimony. I was driven all the more by the shocking experiences within the ghetto walls to be constantly on the lookout, wherever I could, sketch pad in hand.

Of course we were often in danger and had to use the greatest caution in drawing, hiding from the SS men who were spread out all over the town, keeping to attics or somewhere in the crowd. Fritta, Ungar, and often Bloch and I were so oppressed by the horrible surroundings that we devoted ourselves to our 'office duties' in the day and then night after night gathered in our darkened workroom, where our sketches matured as a cycle. ❞ Leo Haas, a well-known Czech artist

BARACKENBAU

Fritta's artwork

Fritta used entirely different art styles for his official and secret work. His print above was done to accompany an official report about the progress of the camp. This realistic and impersonal style gives a sense of hard work, order, and efficiency. The carpenters look strong, healthy, and well fed. Their faces, turned away or in shadow, give no sense of their individuality or feelings.

In stark contrast, the camp's true conditions are plain to see in Fritta's smudgy ink drawing below. People huddle in every available space in every building. They stare out, hunched, hollow-eyed, and downcast, their misery hard to ignore.

△ **Building barracks**
Bedrich Fritta

▽ **Life in Terezín**
Bedrich Fritta

Ghetto Life

The Nazis appointed a Jewish Council of Elders to run life in Theresienstadt. This council was in charge of housing, work, health, food, transport, water, finance, children, and free-time activities. In reality, the Nazis issued daily orders that the council had to obey without question. Any offenses were severely punished.

△ **Members of the camp command**
Leo Haas
Inmates had to take off their hats to passing uniformed Nazi soldiers.

Curfew and Confinement

During the first six months of the camp, Czech civilians still lived in Theresienstadt. The Nazis did not want the Jewish inmates to have any contact with either the townspeople or themselves, so they limited where the inmates could go and locked them in at night.

Prohibitions and Punishments

    The hopes for life in the work camp gradually disappear with the wave of prohibitions and orders issued daily: men are forbidden to meet with women; it is forbidden to write home; contact with the Gentile (non-Jewish) population is prohibited; smoking is punished; everybody must be close-shaven; nobody is allowed to walk on the sidewalks, and every uniformed person must be saluted. It is forbidden to go apart from the work group, to leave one's lodgings after curfew, to use the shops, to sing or whistle in the street, to collect horse chestnuts or pick field flowers.

    The prisoners have to hand in money, stamps and writing paper, cigarettes and tobacco, canned foods, medicines, and many other things. They are punished by ten to fifty blows with a cane for small offenses, for larger ones by several months' imprisonment as well. Punishment by beating is frequent and must be carried out by the prisoners themselves.

Josef Polák, a Czech who worked in the ghetto's record-keeping office

Terezín was a powerless community beset by fears and oppressed by ruthless and maddened tyrants.

Bedrich Lederer

Nazi Behavior

    The Nazis behaved like different sorts of animals. They fenced us in. They left the village green in Terezín for the *Kommandantur* and for the house of the *Kommandatur*. They threw the officers into the barracks to see if Jews were smoking cigarettes or if they had anything smuggled in.

Hana Pravda

▷ **View of Terezín**
Bedrich Fritta
This picture shows how crowded the town became. The building with the flag on the corner of the square was the SS headquarters. The entire square was fenced and out-of-bounds to the Jewish inmates.

Housing

Initially, everyone was housed in barracks. Men were separated from women and young children. Dozens of people shared a room with no privacy and scarcely any space to store belongings. There was constant noise, the stink of people who rarely had a chance to bathe, and persistent bedbugs, fleas, and lice.

△ **The exterior of the Dresden barracks today**
Some of the eleven gigantic barracks were renamed after German towns, such as Hanover, Hamburg, Dresden, and Magdeburg.

Rooms for Men and Women

" Men were sent to the Sudeten Barracks, a large three-story building at the periphery of the town. It had been a storehouse for uniforms. The rooms were totally bare; naked lightbulbs hung here and there from the ceiling; concrete floors, barred windows. Everywhere three-tiered bunks, nailed together, with mattresses filled with wood shavings and pillows of the same kind.

The women, separated from the men, were housed in the Hamburg and Dresden Barracks. They were gigantic, three-storied buildings, covering an entire block, with high steep roofs. The rectangular plan of the building included two or three gigantic courtyards surrounded by arcades. These open arcades formed the corridors that led to the lodgings, most large rooms, a few larger halls.

Some of the larger rooms had large tiled cooking stoves that were in almost constant use. At every corner of the square there was a staircase and washrooms with taps and washbasins. Most people used their bowls [to wash in] after having drunk their coffee from them. The courtyards themselves were always crowded. Here people lined up for rations—their children played ball or soccer—fetched bread, delivered coal; there people stood in a tight circle around a coffin, a funeral.

The women in their barracks had no wooden bedsteads; the vaulted ceilings there were too low. They spread their shavings-filled mattresses one next to the other on the floor, which left only a small space to climb into bed. " **Norbert Troller**

▷ **Bunk beds**
František M. Nagl
Those who shared the cramped space of triple bunk beds like these were better off than the many inmates who had to sleep on cold stone floors.

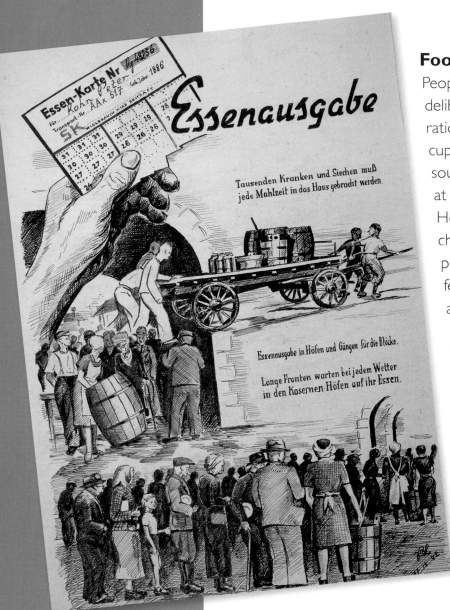

Food

People were always hungry. The Nazis deliberately starved them. Food was rationed and always the same: a morning cup of black coffee; watery vegetable soup, a potato, and a half-loaf of bread at noon; and more soup for dinner. Heavy workers received double rations; children had more than adults, and old people were given the least. Within a few months of arrival, most people lost a third of their weight.

Inmates did whatever they could to get extra food—trading their few remaining belongings, stealing supplies, or smuggling in produce from the gardens. Lucky inmates occasionally received food packages from friends outside or from the Red Cross, when mail was permitted.

◁ **Food distribution**
Peter Löwenstein
This official illustration shows how the food system operated. People lined up in barracks with ration cards and bowls for food served from barrels.

Cooking for Thousands of People

❝ I worked in the kitchen, which was always at that time the place to be—'kitchen' meant working practically in the dungeons, in the cellars, which were equipped with enormous containers, where we were cooking for 5,000 at a time, maybe 10,000. The cooking consisted of soup, sometimes a potato and sometimes a dumpling. All this had been organized to its highest efficiency. People were standing outside in the line three times a day with tickets or a little block of tickets to be clipped. We in the kitchen were standing behind the containers with a ladle and everyone filing past.

The very, very old people filing past always said, 'Please, miss, from the bottom.' This meant that maybe there was a piece of potato or something floating or something down there rather than just liquid. ❞ Zdenka Ehrlich

I heard some people tried to alleviate this ache [of hunger] by sucking their buttons, in the hope that would con the brain into believing they were actually eating something.

Steven Frank, a Dutch schoolboy

Some Ruses for Getting Extra Food

❝ We arranged a little thieving gang. When they unloaded sugar, which came in sacks, they gradually emptied a little from each sack into another sack and I had to transport it in small portions to a room in the station. The same with potatoes and coal and whatever else arrived. Then, later on, we shared it all out. ❞ Aron Sloma

❝ We used to go out, under guard, to a plot where vegetables were grown, to work on this patch. While it was a change from our prison-like life, it did mean the risk of being caught when we tried to smuggle the odd potato or turnip back in the evening to our home. ❞
Arnold Jakubovic, a Czech schoolboy

❝ The Germans had to import food for the prisoners. Wagonloads of potatoes would arrive and we were woken up in the middle of the night to unload them. I used to go and unload potatoes in the baggiest pair of trousers you have ever seen, which were tied at the bottom. By the time I came back, I would have forty pounds of potatoes on me. ❞
Peter Frank, a Czech schoolboy

▽ **Metamorphosis**
Pavel Fantl
This cartoon vividly shows how, in the space of four years, a well-fed, well-dressed arrival with a bulging rucksack and warm bedding was starved and reduced to rags.

Everyone to Work

The Council of Elders assigned work—heavy, ordinary, or light—to everyone over the age of fifteen. They tried to match jobs with people's skills. Trained craftsmen, such as plumbers, bricklayers, and joiners worked in construction or maintenance. Some people worked in tailoring or metal workshops or offices. Others worked in transport. Laborers worked in mines or built sewers or laid the new railway spur into the town.

How Jobs Were Allocated for Young People

△ **Cleaning the square**
Ferdinand Bloch
Even old people, if they were fit enough, were given jobs.

> In the mornings, we had to report for work. I was always late. I could not get up. This can easily be explained. I couldn't face it, and if you can't face a job, you tend not to get up. This was a mistake because the good jobs went first. The good jobs were in the kitchen. The second good jobs were working outside the ghetto in the gardens growing vegetables, but I never got up early enough for that and I ended up being like an apprentice as a builder plumber. I made and fitted hinges, locks, and keys. **Frank Bright, a German youth**

▽ **Return from work**
Bedrich Fritta

Women's Work

Women worked in the kitchens, peeling potatoes, sweeping rooms and courtyards, doing laundry or working in offices, hospitals, or with children.

Work in the Hospital

" My mother volunteered to go and work in the camp hospital laundry—this was a highly infectious area, but it meant she had access to hot water and this meant that, when nobody was looking, she could wash her children's clothes. She could also wash adults' clothes and barter that for extra food. " Steven Frank

The Mica-Slate Splitting Workshop

" It was a workshop within a large barrack, where mica-slate was split very fine, until it was like paper. We sat in groups of twelve at long tables, bent over the work all day long, and gave it all the strength we had. The summer was unbelievably hot, the barrack hot and sweltering. The women talked about home. " Gerty Spies, a German writer

▽ **Splitting mica**
Malvina Schalkova
Mica absorbs high heat without burning, so it was used to insulate electrical equipment in German warplanes. Splitting mica was a nasty, dusty job, which caused rashes and coughs.

△ **Gardening**
Helga Weissová-Hošková
Fruit and vegetables were grown exclusively for Nazi consumption or for sale, not for the camp inmates.

△ **Gardens in the moat**

Work for Young People

Young fit people grew vegetables and fruit in the town's grassy moat and on nearby farms. The council thought this work would be useful training for them for the future.

Life as a Gardener

❝ We converted the soil between the fortifications into very good gardens. That part of Bohemia is very fertile. It has a very good climate—hard winters, very warm summers—and sufficient water. Anything that you plant will grow. We grew all manner of vegetables, and the place was full of apple trees, pear trees, cherries, and apricots. We had fruit year round, because the apples would keep. During the winter, we made straw covers for the greenhouses, so we were occupied all year. Ostensibly, we were supposed to be producing food for the Germans. We were delivering cartloads, wagons pulled by two horses to the Germans, but not very much reached them. ❞ Peter Frank

The Fake Bank

As part of the pretense that the camp ran its own affairs, the Nazis set up a bank in Terezín's former town hall. They named it the Bank of the Jewish Autonomy. The bank issued special camp paper money and savings books and gave people cash wages for their work.

However, the money was totally worthless outside the camp. People now had to pay for once-free showers, for concerts, and at the café. They had to pay a fifty-crown deposit to borrow a book from the camp library. They could also buy things in specially set-up shops that were intended to deceive any outside visitors.

▽ **Ghetto one-hundred crown (Krone) bill**
The picture on the bill shows Moses holding the two stone tablets with the Ten Commandments. Ironically his hand is covering the commandment that reads in Hebrew, "Thou shall not kill."

▽ **Savings book**
False savings, which people could never actually access, were credited to everyone's saving books once a month.

Illness and Disease

Overcrowding, filthy water supplies, vermin, unhygienic bathrooms, and lack of washing facilities led to frequent outbreaks of diseases, including typhoid and scarlet fever. Constant lack of food weakened people, so they fell ill easily and failed to get better. And many old people were already sick and feeble when they arrived.

Hospitals and Health Care

Doctors set up a makeshift hospital for 1,000 patients, using equipment sent from German and Czech Jewish hospitals and doctors' offices that the Nazis had closed down. Every barracks also had a sick bay. However, the only medicines that the Nazis permitted were those that new arrivals brought with them. These were confiscated and given to a central pharmacy. Many world-renowned medical specialists among the inmates performed skilled operations. However, people often died soon afterward of untreated infections for want of the necessary medicines.

▽ **In medical attendance**
Leo Haas

The Fear of Typhus Epidemics

66 The Germans were terrified of typhus. The Germans knew that bugs don't recognize who is Jewish and who is not, and they were very anxious that doctors who were sent to Theresienstadt took a lot of medicines with them. 99 Hana Pravda

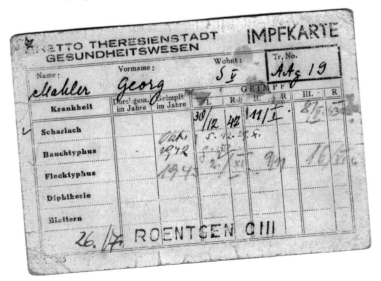

We had about one doctor for every ten people and we had dentists.

Hana Pravda

◁ **Vaccination card**
Some people were vaccinated against highly infectious diseases such as typhoid and scarlet fever.

Disease and Death

The number of sick grew as living conditions worsened. With never enough doctors, nurses, or medicines, more and more people died. A total of 34,647 people died in the camp of starvation or disease.

The Experience of a Typhoid Sufferer

" A typhoid epidemic has seized the ghetto and it has spread disastrously. In our room of twenty-five, a few girls have become ill. After a while, I also contracted typhoid. I am fourteen years old. I was put into isolation. My ward had been a storeroom—a dark place with an arched ceiling and closed external shutters, where day and night only a bare lightbulb shone. Being here was cause enough for despair. Fifty ill people lived, suffered, and were dying here. Children and young and old women refilled vacant beds whenever anyone died. The still-warm bed was taken by a new patient. There was no medication, not enough nurses, and no one who could even give you water. It only remained to wait for death in isolation. "

Raja Englanderová, a Czech teenager

The Daily Occurence of Death

" One nasty thing I remember was seeing the dead people in front of the houses. Every day the dead were taken out into the streets and laid down. You just saw their feet. Their head was covered but not the feet. In front of each house there were two, three, four, dead. " Jan Hartman

◁ **A Hospital in Terezín**
Jan Ullman
There were eventually four hospitals in Terezín, including one for children. There was also an old people's home.

△ **Caution! Mumps is contagious!**
Karel Fleischmann
Fleischmann was a doctor who was also a talented artist. In his free time, he drew many scenes of life in Theresienstadt.

MAIN CAUSES OF DEATH	
Gastroenteritis	8,628
Malnutrition	6,534
Pneumonia	6,412
Heart disease	4,722
Tuberculosis	1,372
Septicemia	896
Cancer	534
Suicide	259
Typhoid	128
Accident	51
Diphtheria	38

29

Transports

Far worse than hunger, disease, and family separation was the constant fear of transports. Theresienstadt was never the permanent place to stay that inmates hoped. Instead, it proved to be a transit point for transports to death camps farther east. Transports began in December 1941, almost as soon as the camp was set up, and continued until October 1944.

How Transport Lists Were Decided

> " The Elders had to make up the transports of people, not the Germans. They [the Germans] told them, 'We want 5,000 people for this and that date and you have to choose who is going.' It was terrible for those people to choose. They were heartbroken doing this every month. Another 5,000. Then another 5,000. A Jew to do this to another Jew. But they had no choice. "

Edith Baneth

TRANSPORTS

There were 63 transports from Theresienstadt.

Initially 1,000 deportees at a time went on a transport. Later transports carried 2,000 or 5,000 people.

A total of 86,934 people left Theresienstadt on transports east. Fewer than 3,000 survived.

△ **Transport statistics**
Most people from Theresienstadt were sent to death camps such as Treblinka or Auschwitz in Poland. There, they were murdered in gas chambers.

◁ **Registration for a transport**
Karel Fleischmann

To "the East"

No one knew where the transports were headed, only that they went to "the East." The Nazis claimed that transports were going to new settlements. To reinforce this deception, they made deportees write postcards back to remaining inmates, saying they were well, just before they were sent to the gas chambers to die.

Summons to a Transport

❝ The summons to go was a narrow strip of thin paper with a name, a tag number, tomorrow's date (it always came the day before), the time—usually four in the morning—and the place of assembly. Those narrow strips were often distributed only a few hours before departure. There was no time for anything. It was forbidden to be out at night, so on the other side of the ghetto, one's family did not know. ❞

Jana Renée Friesová, a Czech teenager

Privileged Protection

Some people, at least for the first few years, were protected from transports. Those who did work that was deemed indispensable—such as skilled craftsmen, the original work crews and their families, artists, musicians, the heads of the police and fire services—were protected. Mothers and small children, the Council of Elders, prominent German Jews, and the severely ill were also initially protected. By the last transports, scarcely anyone was exempt.

There was a complete lack of information of what they [the Germans] had in mind.

Hana Pravda

Surviving was everything.

Norbert Troller

▽ **Ready for a transport**
Peter Löwenstein

Appeals

At first, people could appeal against being sent on a transport. The Germans made the final decision about who went or not.

Decision Time in the Commandant's Office

“ There is a long line in front of the commandant's office. Everyone of us knows that it is about life or death, that inside there are two SS officers, next to them are two secretaries, and everyone will be questioned by them. Then—and we know that too—the slip of paper will be carefully aimed through the air. If it flies to typewriter Number 1, it means transport—no one knows where to. But it means the end; that we all know. ” **Gerty Spies**

"Going East"

“ On the way out, we knew only the words *going east*. We were kept in the dark. The word *Auschwitz* was sort of hazy. We did not know what was going on; we had no imagination, no image in our mind of what a concentration camp actually looked like. There was no reference to it anywhere, but it was a frightening thing to be in a transport. Because once you were in, the destination was very much unknown and we didn't know anybody who ever came back, ever returned. ” **Zdenka Ehrlich**

The Journey to Auschwitz

“ The train was a freight cattle train. It had no windows, but narrow slits in the side allowed some air to come in. There was just enough room in our wagon for all to sit or lie down on the floor. We were provided with food for one day and some old blankets. The trip was slow and, at times, the train stood for hours. No one knew where we were going or how long it would take.

Our family was together, so that we provided some comfort for each other. It was late at night when we arrived. The doors of the cattle car were opened from the outside. They had been sealed securely on departure from Theresienstadt. Uniformed German SS guards were issuing orders: 'Quickly, out of the train and line up in rows of five along the track.' ” **John Freund**

No one could be certain when his turn would come to be deported to the East.

Zdenek Lederer

▽ **Transport to the East**
Leo Haas

When you arrived at the railway station, there were the cattle wagons ready. The SS were there. Our people were helping the people into the wagons.

Edith Baneth

The Aftermath of a Transport

" In the days following the departure of a transport (each containing about 1,000 people), quarters and bunks around were empty. We walked around like phantoms. The sense of loss and sadness was terrible. After each new transport, new occupants moved into the vacated bunks. They were not accepted kindly, but often with animosity. After all, they were taking the place of dear friends. The newcomers were intruders, foreigners. "

Jana Renée Friesová

The Ghetto Grows

In June 1942, Czech civilians still living in Theresienstadt were expelled from their houses to make way for thousands of elderly, wealthy, or prominent German and Austrian Jews. The Nazis told these Jews that, in exchange for signing over their assets, they could go to the town as a safe haven for the rest of the war. The truth proved very different.

The Effects of the Rapid Population Growth

△ **German Jews about to board a train for Theresienstadt**
Many people packed ball gowns, furs, and jewelry, thinking they were going to a fancy spa.

❝ July 18, 1942—Shabbat
Transports arrive daily in this city which can normally absorb 3,000 people. A chess game! Today there are 30,000 people. There are days when 2,000 people arrive at once. Problems of disinfection, eradication of lice, space, creating beds, a colorful mosaic of life and death.

July 19, 1942
So many contrasts in life here. In the yard, a cabaret with singers and in the houses the old and sick and dying. The young are full of desire to have a full life and the old are left without a place and without rest.

July 20–21, 1942
It will not be possible to use the toilets, for the sewers are stopped up.

August 10, 1942

If you wander through the street of the ghetto, you encounter old men and women. They go to receive food and frequently get lost on the way. A transport has arrived with 1,450 people from Prague. They sent sixteen-year-old youths as laborers. The ghetto is too full.

August 11, 1942

The rooms are full. The people roll about on the floor. They lack utensils. The dead lie among the living for an entire day, the sick on floors of stone. The walls drip with moisture. At noon, the people that live in these houses stand in the courtyards. The food gets cold. Sometimes it rains.

August 13, 1942

The city is too full. Despite this, a transport with 1,000 people is expected tomorrow. No one knows if there will be places for these people, where they will put them.

August 14, 1942

The food is tasting better now because new potatoes have arrived. There isn't enough space for the people who are already here. No one knows what will be done for the people who come tomorrow. They want to settle them in attics. Three transports will go eastward.

△ **Old woman with a bowl**
Otto Ungar

▽ **Life in the attic**
Otto Ungar
Hundreds of old people were crowded into filthy attics, without lighting or washing facilities. They slept on the floor and were given no care or help. Many died within weeks of arrival.

The clock ticks well.

Siegfried Seidl, camp commandant (when told of the high mortality rate)

▽ **Funeral wagon with corpses**
Bedrich Fritta
A wagon leaves the camp for a mass grave. Mourners were not allowed beyond the town gate. By the fall of 1942, so many people were dying that a crematorium—forbidden by Jewish tradition—with four furnaces was quickly built.

> **August 25, 1942**
>
> Three transports will go. Rumor has it that they are deciding how many Jews will come, at what pace the old will die. Much work and sadness fills the soul.
>
> **August 26, 1942**
>
> Night. A summer's night. The barrack sleeps. People sleep. Worries leave them. They have passed to the world of dreams. The electric lightbulbs cast their gloomy light on the hallways. A large shadow looms over the house, over the ghetto, over the world. People sleep and dream of a better tomorrow.
>
> **September 5, 1942**
>
> The number of dead—one, then ten. After that, tens, fifties, sixties. The number grew and grew. It became nearly one hundred per day. Now it has reached 130. It's hot here, as it never was before, and there is no one to dig graves. The struggle for life is immense. A disease means a worse classification and the possibility of a summons to a transport. "

Gonda Redlich, the Czech organizer of youth welfare in the ghetto

Death and Deportations

By July 1942, Jews over the age of sixty-five made up a third of the camp's inmates and by September, more than half. Overcrowded housing, poor sanitation, illness, and lack of food weakened many already frail elderly people. By October, more than 10,000 of them had died. During September and October, 23,000 people over the age of sixty were deported to their deaths at either Treblinka or Auschwitz.

△ **A transport leaves the ghetto**
Bedrich Fritta

Old People's Transports

❝ Ten thousand sick, crippled, dying, all of them over sixty-five years old. I am too exhausted to stand the sight of misery and suffering again. The old people's transport, the young people cannot volunteer [to take their place]. Children have to let their parents go off and can't help them. Why do they want to send these defenseless people away? If they want to get rid of us young people, I can understand that; maybe they are afraid of us, don't want us to give birth to any more Jewish children. But how can these old people be dangerous? If they had to come to Terezín, isn't that enough? Can't they let them die in peace here? After all, these old people can't hope for anything else. Half of them will die in the sluice and in the train. ❞ Helga Weissová-Hošková, a teenage Czech artist

△ **Portrait of an old woman**
Bedrich Fritta

Children

The Jewish Council made sure children had more living space and better food than adults. Although the Nazis officially banned teaching, children had secret classes in most subjects, often disguised as songs, plays, games, or storytelling. Life was made as normal as possible, but children were still often hungry, ill, and afraid.

△ **The former girls' home today**
Girls age eight to sixteen lived in this building. Thirty girls were housed in each room, organized by age and nationality.

Children's Homes

Once the townspeople had left, boys moved into the former school and girls into the former military headquarters. Children were housed by age group in separate rooms. A room leader, often a teacher, was in charge of each group, organizing classes and trying to keep the children clean, healthy, entertained, disciplined, and as happy as possible.

If we can only save the young ... The Jewish people will have biological continuity.

Jakob Edelstein, Jewish Council elder

Life in the Boys' Home from April 1942 to 1944

> We were given talks by teachers, we played games and had our chores, and were under strict discipline. We played chess, Twenty Questions, and at times, we put on plays. We published a newsmagazine once a week. At certain times, we were allowed to go out of school to walk around or to visit our parents.
>
> In Room Nine, we formed intense friendships. We discussed everything, even held Ping-Pong championships. So life went on. We were hungry and at times sick, but we did not complain.

John Freund

△ **Cover of *Kamarád* (Friend) magazine**
Children handwrote and illustrated twenty-two issues of this magazine.

Life in the Boys' Home from September 1944

> We had no school. We could do what we liked. We had packs of cards, not complete of course, but enough cards to play patience and snap. There were a few chess sets about. There was another game we called football. We used buttons. The large buttons were the players and the smaller button was the ball and we would flick the bigger button on to the smaller button and we'd make a goalpost. Steven Frank

A Matron's Job

> To be a matron in a home meant to be on call twenty-four hours a day, to sleep with the children, to get up at night and wake Rudy to prevent him from wetting his pallet, half an hour later Charles for the same reason, to rinse Mike's inflamed eyes, to give a pill to Freddy, to change Tommy's compress. There were many sick children in every room. Here again, the matron had to sit down at the bunk of a restless sleeper and stroke his brow to prevent him from waking and frightening the others with his cries. During the day she had to look after the children's cleanliness, their rations, distribute them, get a voucher for shoe repairs, take a child to the doctor, get hold of some medicine, beg for a little yeast in the bakery, the best medicine for all the numerous sties, in short — care for the children's mental and physical well-being. "

Irma Lauscherová, a Czech teacher

▽ **Weekly menu for the children's kitchen**
Charlotte Verešová, who wrote the menu shown below in her diary, commented, "This menu doesn't look so bad, but it is impossibly cooked and the soups are the same every day. They look like water from washing the floors."

	LUNCHES	SUPPERS
Monday	soup, millet	small loaf of bread
Tuesday	soup, potatoes, turnips	soup
Wednesday	soup, potatoes, goulash	small loaf of bread
Thursday	soup, barley	sausage, soup
Friday	soup, barley	bun
Saturday	soup, potatoes, turnips	soup
Sunday	soup, bun with cream sauce	20 gms margarine, teaspoon of jam

▽ **Karel is sick and reads aloud**
Unknown artist

MEITNER EVA

skup IV. hun

△ **Seder**
Eva Meitner

Friedl Dicker-Brandeis

Friedl Dicker-Brandeis, an Austrian Jew, was already an established artist when she was deported to Theresienstadt in December 1942. She lived in the girls' home and secretly taught more than six hundred children to draw, paint, sew, and make puppets. She organized an exhibition of children's work in the cellar of the home.

Before she was transported to Auschwitz in 1944, she hid two suitcases containing more than 4,000 children's works. Today, these are on show at the Jewish Museum in Prague.

▷ **Collage**
Alice Sittig

Drawing Lessons with Friedl Dicker-Brandeis

66 I can still see the table in the middle of the room with pencils on it, paintbrushes, colors, and paper. The paper was very poor quality, often waste paper or paper left over from some old package. Each child could draw freely according to his imagination and wishes. This was extraordinary. It gave us a different life, another atmosphere.

Sometimes she brought various papers and I would make collages. We often painted with watercolors or simply sketched. She often brought art books and also postcards of works of art, and she had us imitate famous paintings, either with collage or with watercolor. Or she would bring flowers or some other item—some pots or a few wooden shoes. Once she told us to paint each other, or to paint something that was especially important to us.

She often gave us specific subjects, assigned themes for us to draw. But she would also tell us to use our free imagination, telling us to just paint the place where you wish you were now. Or to paint what you wish for. Then, of course, each child painted something different. 99 **Helga Pollak**

There was something about her way of teaching that made us, for the moment, feel free of care.

Helga Pollak, a Czech teenager

▽ **Collage with signpost to Prague (Praha)**
Unknown artist

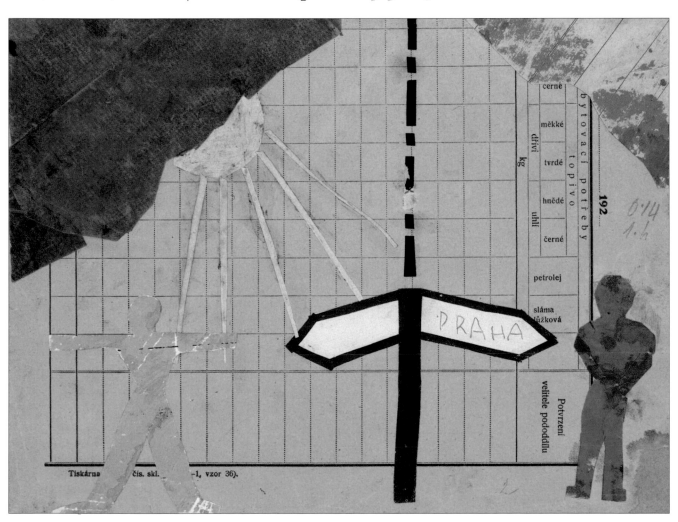

Around me I see the empty beds
the beds of forty-two living boys
until the order came: the expected transport
now they must go

Called by their names one by one
forty-two delicate pairs of freezing legs
formed up in a line, each with his rucksack
now they are gone,

Boys who played and laughed and quarreled
and wept when struck by the thought of
home they wanted to live, were full of
longings imprisoned by the ghetto.

Bare shabby sacks of straw
where still this morning the boys lay
forty-two cheerful boys alive
empty beds

△ **Poem by Paul Aron Sandfort**
The Danish child who wrote this poem
was transported to Theresienstadt
on October 26, 1943, and survived.
He is the third boy from the left in the
photograph on page 50.

△ **Girl about to leave
on a transport**

Children's transports

The Council of Elders managed to protect children younger than twelve from transports until September 1943. Then children too were sent to Auschwitz. Gradually the age limit was lowered, until even infants were deported as well. Fifteen thousand children passed through Theresienstadt. Fewer than one hundred survived. Around 8,000 were sent on transports.

A diary About a Children's Transport

" **Thursday, August 16, 1943**
It's terrible here now. There is a great deal of tension among the older children. They are going to send transports to a new ghetto into the unknown.

Saturday, September 4, 1943
Tomorrow they load the transport. From our room only Zdenka is going so far. They are sending them in several batches. Zdenka is acting very bravely.

Sunday, September 5, 1943
This was a day, but it's all over now. They are already in the sluice. From our room Pavla, Helena, Zdenka, Olila, and Popinka are going. Everyone gave Zdenka something; she's such a poor thing. I gave her a half loaf of bread, a can of meat paste, linden tea, and sugar. At six in the evening they reported for the transport. The parting was hard. After eight in the evening I went to look for Zdenka. She was sitting on her luggage and she cried and laughed at the same time to see someone before she left. I slept all night, but I had terrible dreams and had rings under my eyes in the morning.

Monday, September 6, 1943
I got up at six to see Zdenka again. When I came up to the Hamburg barracks, the last people were just going through the back gate and getting on the train. Everything was boarded up all around so no one could get to them and they could not run away. I jumped over and ran up to the last people going through the gates. I saw the train pulling away. In one of the cars, Zdenka was riding away. "

Helga Kinsky, an Austrian teenager

Culture

Among the inmates were a large number of world-class musicians, composers, and conductors. At first in secret, and later with Nazi approval, musicians performed concerts, opera, and cabarets. Some wrote new works. There were also many famous theater directors and actors who put on plays.

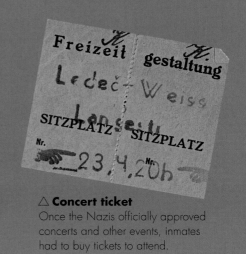

△ **Concert ticket**
Once the Nazis officially approved concerts and other events, inmates had to buy tickets to attend.

Concerts and Cabarets

"" There were moments that seemed strangely magnified by a feeling of blissful make-believe amid an otherwise cold reality. I remember how overjoyed we were one day by the music of an accordion that someone had smuggled into the barracks. Everyone huddled together in the poorly lit, freezing room, and for a while we forgot our hurt as we listened to the tunes.

Or I remember how we gathered at night in a cramped storage cellar to listen to Karel Svenk's *Cheers to Life,* Terezín's first underground production. This was a stinging political cabaret, and one of our own men stood guard at the door in case any SS appeared. ""

Alfred Kantor, a Czech artist

Culture was one of those things they couldn't take from us.

Helga Weissová Hošková

▽ **A performance in a dormitory**
Bedrich Fritta

◁ **A lecture in the Sudeten Barracks**
Karel Fleischmann
Renowned university professors gave hundreds of lectures on science, law, literature, philosophy, music, and medicine. Listeners had to stand, as there were no chairs.

Lectures and Literary Events

> " We had shows almost every night in the attics and in the cellars. We had four pianos—only real professional virtuosos were allowed to play them. There were singing choirs.
>
> You could listen to lectures on the history of art, on physics, on mathematics. Our intellectual life was more intense than ever before. We had books, we had poetry, we had evenings of poetry, and all this worked miracles on the morale of people, I assure you, even if they were hungry. " Hana Pravda, a Czech actress

Brundibár—A Children's Opera

The most famous opera composed in Theresienstadt was *Brundibár*, a children's opera. The story tells how a brother and sister need to buy milk for their sick mother. The children and their animal friends earn a few coins by singing, but Brundibár, an evil organ grinder, steals their money. The children chase Brundibár to recover it. Brundibár reminded audiences of Hitler, so after the final victory song, they cheered thunderously at the triumph of good over evil.

△ **Poster for *Brundibár***
There were fifty-five performances of this opera, including one for the Red Cross visit (see page 49) and one for the film (see page 54).

△ **Entertainment in a courtyard**
Bedrich Fritta

Nightly Nourishment

Performances took place at night, after work, in attics, barracks, courtyards, and cellars. Some people were too hungry, exhausted, or ill to come. For many others, these entertainments helped them forget, if only for a short while, their dismal daily lives.

△ **Entertainment in a courtyard**
Bedrich Fritta

Food for the Soul

❝ I remember vividly we had performed *Faust* by Goethe and people were sitting with closed eyes, obviously seeing it in their minds in a big theater. Afterward, when we had finished, they came with pieces of margarine, forcing it on us, bread and margarine, and we didn't want to take it, naturally. They said, 'Please, please take it, because you gave us the illusion of the free world.' I can assure you, if anyone is ever in the lurch, poetry, theater, and music are the only answers for survival. ❞

Hana Pravda

What sustained us was culture. I laugh at people who say it is a luxury.

Hana Pravda

45

Beautification

Four hundred sixty-six Danish Jews arrived at Theresienstadt in late 1943. The Danish king requested a Red Cross visit to see their living conditions, since rumors were circulating that Jews were being killed in gas chambers. The Nazis saw the visit as an opportunity to counter these rumors by pretending that the town was a "model Jewish settlement." First, however, they needed to "beautify" it.

Thorough "Beautification"

" It's ridiculous, but it seems that Terezín is to be changed into some sort of spa. The orders are received in the evening, and in the morning everyone's eyes are staring with wonder. Where did this or that thing come from? For three years it never occurred to anyone that streets might be named anything but Q and L. But all of a sudden the Germans had an idea, and overnight signs had to be put on every corner house with the name of the street, and at the corners arrows pointed: To the Park, To the Baths, etc.

The school by the construction headquarters that had served as a hospital up to today was cleared out overnight and the patients put elsewhere while the whole building was repainted, scrubbed up, school benches put in, and in the morning a sign could be seen from afar: 'Boys' and Girls' School.' It really looks fine, like a real school; only the pupils and teachers are missing. That shortcoming is adjusted by a small note on the door: 'Vacation.'

The whole thing was a comedy. We had no idea what it was about.

Edith Baneth

◁ **A Potemkin village**
Bedrich Fritta
Fritta's picture is an acid comment on how Terezín was turned into a sham showcase. A hearse filled with coffins stands in front of false shop fronts, which hide a pile of dead bodies.

> On the square the newly sown grass is coming up, the center is adorned by a big rose plot, and the paths, covered with clean, yellow sand, are lined with rows of newly painted benches. The boards we wondered about for so many days, trying to puzzle out what they were for, were turned into a music pavilion. We even have a café with the fine sign *Kaffeehaus* (coffeehouse).

◁ **The music pavilion**
This pavilion was erected on the town square for concerts on the day of the Red Cross visit.

And all the shops have got new names of firms. The houses will also be painted. The barracks behind Magdeburg where they had the production and processing of mica have become a 'dining hall.' The girls that are specially employed there to heat up the food must wear white caps and aprons.

The physical culture hall was turned into a restaurant with carved furniture, plush chairs in the foyer, and big vases with bouquets. On the second floor there is a library and reading room and little tables on the terrace with colored sunflowers. They have already gotten quite far in painting the houses. Some of the Dutch inmates' rooms have gotten equipment. In two of the barracks, some bunks and shelves were painted yellow and they got blue curtains. In the park in front of the Infants' Home they put up a luxury pavilion with cribs and light-blue quilted covers. In one room there are toys, a carved rocking horse, and so on. Then there is a pool, a merry-go-round, and seesaws. "

Helga Weissová-Hošková

△ **The entrance to the *Sokol* (the physical culture hall) today**

> All the Danes were moved into renovated houses where families were put together, which had never been seen before, because normally men and women were apart. We were in a big room with three families. There were the four of us, a son and his mother, a family with a small child, a single woman, and a single man. We had normal beds, bed linen, and blankets. Outside the house there was a shower room, only cold water, but at least a chance to get a shower, and a little kitchen at the back with a sink and a cooking facility, so people could prepare meals there. **Aron Sloma**

Additional Transports

A few weeks before the visit, there were three transports of 7,500 people altogether. The Nazis wanted to make the camp seem less crowded and to get rid of the sick and frail, especially the 1,200 people with TB (tuberculosis), whose appearance might raise suspicions about malnutrition. A large number of orphans were also sent in these transports, to avoid any questions being raised about where their missing, dead, or deported parents were.

▽ **Cutting down the third level of bunks before the Red Cross visit**
Helga Weissová-Hošková
One tier of bunks was cut down in the dormitory that the Red Cross was going to see, to make the room seem less crowded.

△ **The Red Cross delegation arrives**
Helga Weissová-Hošková
This picture sums up the Nazis' deception. The visitors arrive by car with painting, sweeping, and curtain hanging still in progress. Fresh bread, fruit, and vegetables are all conspicuously in view.

The Red Cross Visit

The Red Cross group was taken on a carefully planned route, along spotless roads with freshly painted houses and well-stocked shops. During their six-hour tour, they saw the bakery, pharmacy, boys' home, and hospital. The Nazi ruse succeeded. The Red Cross reported favorably, commenting that the housing was airy and attractive, food was adequate, and medical supplies were sufficient.

Perfect Stage Management

    In the early morning the women have scrubbed the sidewalks over which the commission will pass. Scouts run ahead and at their command the 'beautifying show' starts working. In one street, the commission—'by chance'—meets a group of girls, marching with rakes shouldered; in another, white-gloved bakers are unloading bread; at the communal center, the orchestra is playing a requiem; and at the exact moment when the commission reaches the sports ground, the ordered goal is shot before an audience that has been ordered to attend.

△ **Children in the park**
A Red Cross visitor took this photograph of apparently well-fed, well-dressed children playing in the park. The hand-picked children had, in fact, been given clothes especially for this occasion.

▽ **Map of Theresienstadt**
The red line on the map plots the route that the Nazis' meticulously planned for the Red Cross visitors.

Fantastic Lies

" In front of the 'grocers'—by chance—fresh vegetables are unloaded and waitresses serve lunch in the spotlessly clean house that has the dining room. Children are riding on the roundabout; the 'bank manager' is smoking a cigar and offers visitors cigarettes. Nobody knows that this very same 'bank manager' has recently been locked up in prison for three months because he was found smoking.

Fantastic lies were told to the members of the commission that day. And they never saw the old sick bays, they did not see the old people's home, they naturally did not see the underground bunkers, the transport department was closed, the transport lists well hidden, nor was the store stuffed full of stolen things shown. No old people, cripples, blind were to be seen anywhere—they were not allowed out into the streets that day, so as not to create a bad impression. " **Josef Polák**

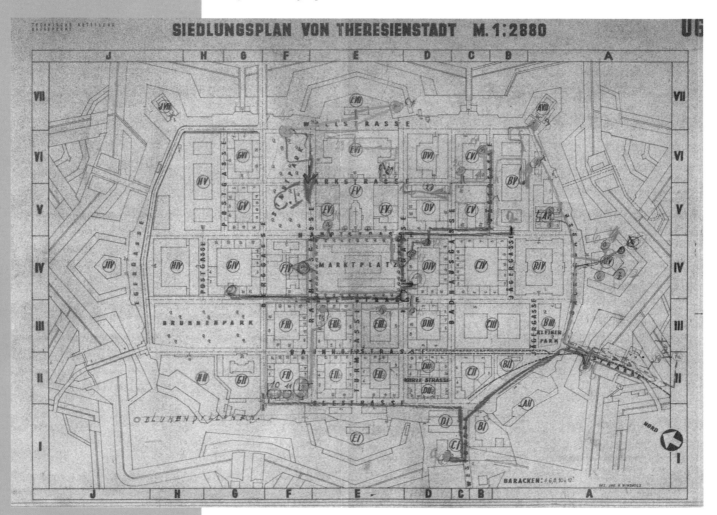

△ **A picturesque courtyard**
Joseph. E. A. Spier
Spier, a Dutch artist, painted eighteen different watercolors of Theresienstadt. These show a spacious, peaceful, cheerful, and apparently normal town, in total contradiction to the grim reality.

Souvenir Books

The Germans asked Joseph Spier, head of the art department, to make picture booklets of Theresienstadt, to give to each of the Red Cross group as a souvenir of their visit. Spier's pictures showed the school, the hospital, the gardens, the square, the bakery, and the main streets. These gave a totally false view of camp life. Dr. Maurice Rossel, the head of the Red Cross group, submitted his copy of the book as part of his evidence, along with a written report and the photographs he took of his visit.

How the Books Were Created

❝ I belonged to a set of painters who had to make the black-and-white prints. I had to paint all the skies one after the other for I don't know how many books. I had to paint light-blue skies to make it look happy. ❞ **Lily Fischl**

We are astonished to find out that the ghetto is a community leading an almost normal existence.

Dr. Maurice Rossel,
the Red Cross

1944 July 17
The Painters' Affair

A few weeks after the Red Cross inspection, four artists—Bedrich Fritta, Ferdinand Bloch, Otto Ungar, and Leo Haas—were told to report to the SS office. The Nazis had somehow discovered that these artists had been drawing in secret and that some of their work had been smuggled out to Switzerland. The artists hurriedly hid the rest of their work.

> **How could you think up such a mockery of reality and draw it?**
>
> SS Captain Rolf Günther

Interrogation

> 66 Günther [an SS captain] questioned me, showing me a study of Jews searching for potato peels and saying, 'How could you think up such a mockery of reality and draw it?' I explained that it was not something I had invented, but what I had happened to see on official duties, and had immediately sketched, in the way that a painter seeks objects to paint. Then came the question, 'Do you really think there is hunger in the ghetto, when the Red Cross did not find any at all?' 99
>
> **Leo Haas, the only one of the four artists to survive**

▽ **Hunger**
Leo Haas
People scrabble in the earth for potato peels. Behind them, starving children reach into the bread cart for any remaining crumbs.

Imprisonment

After questioning, the artists were pushed with gun butts into trucks, where they found their wives and children. They were all taken to the Small Fortress, where the men were put in one cell and the women and children in another.

Torture and Transport

△ **The entrance to the Small Fortress**

> I do not want to recount the suffering we had to endure. Ungar was the first to be sent [to Auschwitz] from the Small Fortress, and Bloch was beaten to death on the spot. Mrs. Ungar and her daughter survived Auschwitz, while Otto Ungar died of typhus, in Buchenwald, after liberation. There remained in the fortress Fritta and I, our wives and little Thomas Fritta. . . .
>
> We two received an indictment for horror propaganda and its dissemination abroad, with a warrant for our arrest that we were to sign voluntarily. . . And which bore the remark 'R.U.' (return not desired). The very next day we rode in cell cars attached to an express train to Auschwitz. Fritta was very feeble and scarcely able to move.

Leo Haas

Auschwitz and After

Fritta soon died of dysentery in Auschwitz. Haas survived and so did his wife, who spent a year in solitary confinement with Tommy, Fritta's son, whom they adopted. Once the war was over, Haas returned to Terezín and found not only his own drawings, undamaged, but also all the works hidden by Ungar, Fritta, and Fleischmann.

▷ **A page from Tommy's book**
Bedrich Fritta
Fritta made a clothbound picture book as a present for his three-year-old son, Tommy. He captioned each drawing in neat lettering. The caption for this picture is "This is not a fairy tale. It's true!"

TO NENÍ POHÁDKA - TO JE PRAVDA!

1944 August–December
A propaganda Film

Having successfully duped the Red Cross, the Nazis decided to make use of the now "beautified" town to make a propaganda film about it. They thought this might be a good way to delude the rest of the world about their treatment of the Jews. They ordered Kurt Gerron, a German inmate and former actor and film director, to direct it.

△ **Kurt Gerron**
Charlotte Burešová

Farcical Filming

    Workdays were properly scheduled for the filming; one knew in advance what would be shot where. There was a sound car, a light car, a spot light, a proper script, and a complete technical staff, the best the ghetto had. . . .

    The attitudes of the Terezín inhabitants varied greatly. A small number pushed forward and wanted absolutely to take part in the film, while the greater part of the people carried out passive resistance and cleared away immediately when they saw people with the white band that had 'Film' printed on it. They could be made to work as extras only by force.

    Gerron began with a shot of the facade of the (fake) bank. After the shots of the bank came the post office, where people were to stand in line at the package window to receive packages that they then had to give up again after the scene had been filmed. People were taken to the SS swimming pool to make the world believe the ghetto had a pool. The fact that the Eger River was closed off right and left by boats filled with SS men was not shown in the film, of course.

▷ **Workshops outside the ghetto and gardening in the fortress moat**
Joseph E. A. Spier
Spier followed the film crew and drew hundreds of sketches of what he saw through the camera's viewfinder between each shot.

▽ **Film and reality**
Bedrich Fritta
In the drawing below, Fritta comments poignantly on the falsity created for the film. A camera focuses on an old man being made up in front of a makeshift screen concealing an anguished skeleton.

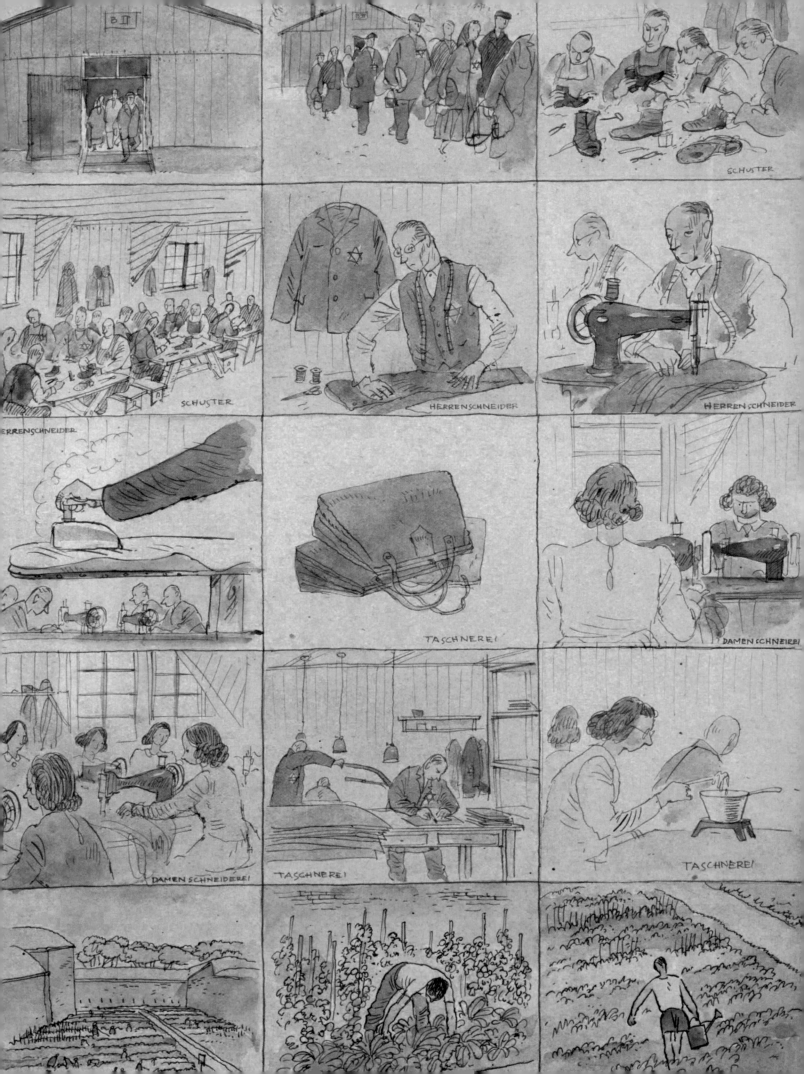

"And the crazy comedy went on. The food rations were
tripled; there was a mass weighing of the inmates, and the
first ten people who were filmed when they went to get their
food had a feast. Outside the ghetto, in a meadow, an open-air
cabaret was held for an audience of 2,000. A marshy meadow
was chosen, where the people had to stand up to their ankles
in water—surely to remind them that they were not here for
pleasure.

The first act of *The Tales of Hoffman* was performed in the
gymnasium, for which inmates had been allowed to make their
own decorations and costumes. In another hall, a symphony
orchestra was filmed. On the terrace, a coffeehouse was
installed, with umbrellas over the tables. In the garden, close-
ups were taken of prominent people from the arts, politics,
and science. Gerron had a very hard job, for not a piece of film did he
see. The director of shooting told him what was good and what was bad.

They continued with the falsifications. A set-up operation in the
hospital, a transport arriving with Rahm [the camp commandant]
personally lifting children from the railway car, an obligatory five-o'clock
tea in the coffeehouse, to the tune of a twelve-piece jazz band, that lasted
until two am. In filming the crèche, the main shots were of a swing and
a toboggan that were sent away again the next day. In the main squares
couples promenaded as a band played, while old people sat on benches.
The camera traveled through the workshops, the carpenter shop, the
shoe shop, and the laundry." Hans Hofer, the film's assistant director

△ **The filmmakers
at work**
The filmmakers were
all professionals.

After Filming Was Finished

Once filming was over, transports intensified, taking 18,402 people to
Auschwitz. Now that the camp's cultural activities had served the Nazis'
hypocritical purposes, Council Elders, musicians, and artists, all previously
exempt from transport, were sent to their deaths. By the end of 1944,
only 11,000 people remained in Theresienstadt, mostly women. The film,
however, was neither edited nor shown before the war ended.

△ **A still from the film**
Apparently well-fed children
lie on beds outside the fake
convalescent home.

**The general well-
being shown by
the film changed
back into the
gray daily life of
Terezín, with its
filth, hunger, and
disease.**

Hans Hofer

The Final Winter of the War

"The Jewish Council's artificially built structure had collapsed. Cooks,
men, doctors, wardens, and our wonderful carers—all had gone.
There were only sick people and even more hunger. The ghetto finally
became a desolate place, just as the Germans had planned."

Jana Renée Friesová

1945 January–May
The End of the War

Throughout 1944, Germany was forced to give up its conquests in Europe. In June 1944, American and English forces landed in France; they liberated Paris in August, then moved east as Soviet forces began moving west. By December, Germany had to defend its own borders. At Theresienstadt and other camps, the Germans started destroying evidence of their crimes.

Burning the Archives

"On the bastions the Germans are burning their archives. Sometimes a bit of paper flies into our garden and we read it. We are not allowed to pick it up, it's true, and a German soldier is guarding us with a gun, but we are curious, of course. Anyway we can't read much of it. Usually there is just a name and date of birth. They are Jewish names. Obviously the Germans are afraid and are trying to smooth over their traces. Why else would they be doing it?"

Charlotte Verešová, a Czech teenager

> **There was this peculiar feeling of elation that war was coming to an end and utter fear that we were going to be gassed.**
>
> Steven Frank

Disposing of the Ashes

"Early one morning, we in the children's home were taken in file to the crematorium, underground. We were made to line up in one great long line in this brick tunnel. Then from the right a little box would appear, big enough for a child to hold. You went to your right, picked up a box, turned to your left, handed it to the next child, and then turned to your right and picked up a box and so it went on for a long time. Each box contained the ashes of the dead of Theresienstadt and, in traditional German fashion, each box had the name of the person whose ashes it contained, their date of birth, where they were born, when they died. From time to time, either upstream or downstream, you would suddenly hear quiet sobbing. It wasn't hysterical crying like when children were taken away. It was subdued grief as somebody held in their hands the ashes—of their mother or father, brother, sister, or friend—briefly before they passed it to the next person." Steven Frank

▽ **The columbarium today**
This is the building where the boxes of ashes were stored.

Death Marches

The Nazis blew up the gas chambers at Auschwitz and, as Soviet troops moved into Poland, evacuated prisoners from the death camps by cattle truck or on forced marches. The prisoners traveled for hundreds of miles toward Germany. Hundreds of thousands died on the way. Fifteen thousand prisoners arrived at Theresienstadt.

▽ **Death-camp prisoners**
Weak and starving, former death-camp prisoners traveled in open trucks, often without food.

A Terrible Train Journey to Theresienstadt

“ The Allies were approaching, so the order came that we must be taken out, right away, at night. We had to run through back streets, because the main roads were full of retreating Germans, waiting with anti-tank weapons for the Allies to come in. We could see that the war was finished and it was only a matter of time, but we asked ourselves, 'Would we survive at this very late hour?' We marched all night and again the following day. The Germans got tired and had to be replaced. They couldn't keep up the march, but we had to. They got food, water, and tea. We got nothing.

They decided to put us in open wagons, one hundred to a wagon, exceptionally overcrowded. No food. No water. No toilet facilities. In some places where we stopped, we were so starving, we ate our own shoes, human flesh, bark of trees, leaves, whatever we could find. We were on that journey for three weeks. You can imagine how many people perished, the cold at night, the terrible battles at night to lie down, one on top of the other. ” **Mayer Hersh, a Pole who survived eight concentration camps**

You reach a point where you either survive or you don't.

Mayer Hersh

Arrival in Theresienstadt

> Suddenly we were in a town. We hadn't been in a town for three years. We had showers, we got clean clothing, we were deloused with a brush, and then we felt rejuvenated. Then we were taken to wooden barracks in the fields. There was a beautiful view of the Sudeten mountains. We didn't have to get up in the morning at five o'clock, for the first time in three years, because there was no work there. I just slept as much as I could. **Ben Helfgott, a Pole**

Liberation

On May 7, 1945, Germany finally surrendered. The next day, the Russian army arrived to liberate Theresienstadt.

The Arrival of the Russians

> For days we had waited nervously, wondering who would liberate us, the Americans or the Russians. When the moment came at last, many prisoners—I among them—ran out onto the street which led from Leitmeritiz to Prague. Everything that separated us from this street and liberty had been trampled down by the prisoners by the time I arrived. Flags and signs welcomed the Russians, who, slowly, in never-ending rows of tanks, passed us. Again and again prisoners broke the rows to offer their hands to the passing soldiers. **Gerty Spies**

Days of Freedom

> Within a matter of days from having looked so arrogant and heroic, they [the Germans] looked downtrodden and disheveled. It was unbelievable. I went over to one dead soldier and took his belt off. It had a buckle which said *Gott mit uns* [God is with us].
>
> After a while, we started going out into the surrounding area and some came back with goods from homes. One came back with a suitcase full of money from a bank. I went out and picked strawberries, just helped myself to what I found.
>
> **Albert Huberman, a Polish survivor**

The Germans disappeared into thin air the night before. That was how we knew it was finished.

Mayer Hersh

▽ **The Russian army liberation of Theresienstadt**
Crowds cheered the arrival of the Russian soldiers.

The Aftermath

△ **A quarantine sign**
Many new arrivals had typhus, which spread not only to the existing inmates but also to towns nearby. The whole town was put under quarantine to contain the epidemic, and everyone was deloused.

❝ Dysentery became rampant. It was a horrific sight. The toilets were overflowing. Wetness everywhere. Disease must have been terrific. Hundreds of people must have died because they ate the wrong food. Fortunately for me, I had TB by this time. I had a temperature and wasn't very hungry, so I didn't eat much and that may have saved me from eating the wrong foods because our stomachs weren't used to it.

After a while, the Russians brought in a team of doctors and nurses and we were examined and taken out of the congested barracks, showered, and put into huge rooms with single beds. We were in Theresienstadt for a while, because we were quarantined until it was deemed we were safe to be let out. Then we were taken by train to Prague and billeted in a school for two weeks.

△ **Repatriation**
Once the quarantine was lifted, survivors left for home or to start a new life elsewhere.

The Russians issued us with an identity card, gave us pocket money for the cinema, transport, the circus, and restaurants. The Czechs were marvelous, providing food for all sorts of refugees milling about all over the place. After two weeks, we were taken to the airport—250 boys and 50 girls—and there were ten British transport planes, with no seats. I sat in the cockpit on a little cockpit seat. We flew over Germany. Below us was devastation. Everything was flattened. ❞ **Alfred Huberman**

The Legacy

After the war, Theresienstadt was named Terezín once more. Gradually, people came to live in the town again. Today, there are almost 2,000 inhabitants, and a few shops and cafés.

The barracks and other large buildings were left locked and abandoned. However, in the past twenty years, the former children's home and one of the barracks have been restored and opened as museums.

These memorials, along with archives of documents, the painters' and children's artwork, and survivors' testimonies, ensure that what happened at Terezín will never be forgotten.

△ **A cell in the Small Fortress**
The Small Fortress opened to the public in 1994. Visitors can see inside the cell blocks where prisoners were held, the washrooms, an operating theater, and the execution yard. An accompanying exhibition explains the history of the fortress as a political prison.

△ **The former Magdeburg Barracks**
In 1997, this refurbished barracks opened as a museum. It has exhibitions about art, music, theater, and literature in the ghetto, as well as a reconstruction of a dormitory.

△ **The National Cemetery**
A National Cemetery was created in 1946 for the remains of 10,000 people who had died in the Small Fortress, the ghetto itself, or the nearby forced-labor camp.

△ **The Jewish Cemetery**
Jews cremated at Terezín are commemorated with a stone menorah— a seven-branched candelabrum, one of the oldest symbols of the Jewish people.

Timeline

1934

August Hitler declares himself Führer of Germany.

1938

March Hitler enters Austria; anti-Jewish laws are imposed.

September Nazi Germany occupies Sudetenland.

November 9 *Kristallnacht:* anti-Jewish riots across Germany, synagogues are destroyed and Jewish cemeteries, shops, and hospitals are vandalized.

1939

March 15 Germany occupies Czechoslovakia and establishes the Protectorate of Bohemia and Moravia.

August 31 Germany invades Poland.

September 3 Great Britain and France declare war on Germany.

1940

March Czech Jews are banned from working in commerce, transport, advertising, or banking.

April Czech Jews are banned from work as doctors, vets, and lawyers.

1941

September 18 Czech Jews are ordered to wear a yellow star.

September 27 Reinhard Heydrich, a leading Nazi, becomes head of the protectorate.

October 10 Nazis decide to turn Terezín into a Jewish ghetto and rename the town Theresienstadt.

October 17 Theresienstadt is proposed as a transit camp to the East.

December 4 The first transport of Prague Jews arrives at Theresienstadt. By the end of the month, there are 7,350 inmates.

1942

January 9 The first transport from Theresienstadt is sent to Riga.

January 20 The Wannsee Conference: Nazi leaders agree on plans for "The Final Solution." Theresienstadt is chosen as a camp for elderly and prominent Jews from Germany and Austria.

May 27 Heydrich is ambushed near Prague; he dies on June 4.

June The Czech inhabitants of Theresienstadt are expelled, and the town is turned over to the Jewish Council of Elders.

June 2 The first elderly Jews from Berlin arrive at Theresienstadt.

June 20 The first Jews from Vienna arrive at Theresienstadt.

July The population at Theresienstadt rises to 43,000.

August 24 Construction begins on a rail spur to Theresienstadt.

September Crematorium construction begins.

September 18 Theresienstadt's population reaches 58,491. During September, 3,941 people die.

October 2 The first Theresienstadt transport is sent to Auschwitz.

1943

January Theresienstadt's population thins with mass deportations to Auschwitz.

April 1 The first Dutch Jews arrive.

April 23 The Bank of Jewish Autonomy opens.

June 1 The first train arrives at Theresienstadt on the new track.

September 5 5,000 are sent to the "family camp" at Auschwitz.

October 5 466 Danish Jews arrive at Theresienstadt.

November 11 A twenty-four-hour census of the entire ghetto is taken.

December 5,007 people are sent to the family camp at Auschwitz. The beautification program begins.

1944

January 2,000 more Dutch Jews arrive.

March 8 3,792 prisoners in the family camp at Auschwitz are sent to the gas chambers.

May 15 7,500 people are sent to the family camp at Auschwitz.

June 23 Visit from the International Red Cross delegation

July 17 The painters' affair

July 6,500 people in the family camp at Auschwitz are liquidated. The Soviet army advances. Death marches begin.

August 16–September 11 Shooting of the propaganda film

September 20 2,081 more Dutch Jews arrive.

September 29–October 28 Eleven transports to Auschwitz, of 18,000 people, leaving only 11,000 people in Theresienstadt, including all the Danes. Seventy percent of those that remain are female.

November 11 Destruction of urns containing ashes. The ashes are dumped in the nearby river.

November 26 Dismantlement of Auschwitz is ordered.

1945

February 5 1,210 inmates leave for safety to Switzerland.

March 11 1,000 Hungarian Jews arrive.

April 15 The Swedish Red Cross transfers 423 Danish prisoners to freedom in Sweden.

April 17 The Nazi archives are burned.

April 20 2,000 prisoners, evacuated from eastern concentration camps, arrive. 15,000 more arrive in the following two weeks. A typhus epidemic breaks out.

April 30 Hitler commits suicide.

May 2 The International Red Cross takes control of Theresienstadt.

May 5 The last SS men abandon their posts at Theresienstadt.

May 7 Germany surrenders.

May 8 The Soviet army liberates the 30,000 inmates of Theresienstadt.

May 10 The Soviet army takes control of Theresienstadt.

May 14–28 The residents are kept in quarantine.

May 28 Repatriation begins and is complete by August.

Glossary

Aryan people of Indo-European stock. The Nazis used this term to mean non-Jewish white people, who were tall with blond hair and blue eyes

concentration camp a prison for large numbers of inmates, using as few guards and at little cost as possible. Prisoners often had to work incredibly hard and received only a minimum of food.

Council of Elders the governing body of the Jewish community at Theresienstadt, set up and controlled by the Nazis

crematorium a large oven for burning dead bodies

death camp a camp where the Nazis killed people in gas chambers, mostly attached to concentration camps. Death camps included Auschwitz, Chelmno, Treblinka, Sobibor, and Majdanek, all in Poland.

death marches Toward the end of the war as the Soviet army advanced, the Germans began to retreat. They forced thousands of concentration camp inmates on long marches, often without food. Thousands died.

Final Solution the Nazi term for wiping out the Jews

ghetto part of a town with walls and gates separating Jews from the rest of the population

Nazi short for National Socialist, the name of Hitler's political party

prominent a Nazi term for Jews who were given better housing than other inmates and initial protection from transports because of some privileged status

quarantine People in quarantine are kept isolated from other people because they have or might have a disease that they could pass on.

repatriation when people return to their own country

sluice (*Schleuse*) nickname for the area in Theresienstadt where new arrivals registered and were systematically robbed of their belongings

SA (*Sturmabteilung*) a paramilitary division of the Nazi party, usually translated as *stormtroopers*

SS (*Schutzstaffel*) Hitler's special, ruthless Nazi force, who wore black shirts as part of their uniform

typhus a dangerous illness transmitted by lice

Sources

The extracts in this book were taken from the following sources:

Dutlinger, Anne D., ed. *Art, Music, and Education as Strategies for Survival: Theresienstadt, 1941–45.* New York: Herodias, 2001.
  Extracts by Helga Pollak and Paul Aron Sandfort

Ehrmann, František, Otta Heitlinger, and Rudolf Iltis, eds. *Terezín.* Prague: Council of Jewish Religious Communities in Czech Lands, 1965.
  Extracts by Leo Haas, Hans Hofer, Irina Lauscherová, Josef Polák, Charlotte Verešová, and Helga Weissová-Hošková

Friedman, Saul S., ed. (translated by Laurence Kutler).
The Terezín Diary of Gonda Redlich. Lexington, KY: University Press of Kentucky, 1992.

Friesová, Jana Renée (translated by Elinor Morrisby and Ladislav Rosendorf). *Fortress of My Youth: Memoir of a Terezín Survivor.* Madison: University of Wisconsin Press, 2002.

Freund, John. *Spring's End.* Azrieli Foundation, 2007. (You can download this book and other memoirs of the Holocaust at www.azrielifoundation.org.)

Oral testimonies of survivors from the Imperial War Museum Sound Archives (www.iwm.org.uk); the numbers in parantheses are the Sound Archive number:
  Edith Baneth (17474), Frank Bright (16841), Zdenka Ehrlich (8942), John Fink (16594), Lily Fischl (9161), Peter Frank (16690), Steven Frank (22600), Jan Hartman (18557), Ben Helfgott (9165), Mayer Hersh (9738), Albert Huberman (18050), Arnold Jacubovic (16695), Freddie Knoller (9092), Hana Pravda (9107), John Silberman (18672), Aron Sloma (23206)

Lederer, Zdenek (translated by K. Weisskkopf). *Ghetto Theresienstadt.* London: Edward Goldstone, 1953.

Spies, Gerty. *My Years in Theresienstadt: How One Woman Survived the Holocaust.* New York: Prometheus Books, 1997.

Troller, Norbert (translated by Susan E. Cernyak-Spatz). *Theresienstadt: Hitler's Gift to the Jews.* Chapel Hill: University of North Carolina Press, 1991.

Index

Acknowledgments

akg-images pp. 7, 9. Beit Theresienstadt p. 38c. bpk/Franz Weber p. 34. © MUDr. Radim Bureš p. 1. Deutsches Historisches Museum, Berlin p. 6. © Art Collection, Ghetto Fighters' Museum, Israel p. 25; © Photo Archive, Ghetto Fighters' Museum, Israel p. 42. © Helga Weissová-Hošková p. 26t. Jüdisches Museum Berlin pp. 17b, 19, 24b, 35b, 36, 37t, 37b, 43b, 45, 46, 54b © Tomáš Fritta-Haas. Image bank WW2—J. Spier collection p. 55 © Peter Spier. Jewish Museum in Prague Photo Archive pp. 12, 21, 24t, 26t, 30; Terezín Children's Drawing Collection 40t, 40b, 41; 44, 50b; 54t © MUDr. Radim Bureš. Collection of Museum of Jewish Heritage—A Living Memorial to the Holocaust, New York pp. 22; 31 Gift of Herman and Gerda Korngold; 52 © Tomáš Fritta-Haas. Neil Thomson pp. 2–3, 4–5, 10, 11, 20, 38t, 47, 53t, 53c, 57, 61. Památník Terezín (The Terezín Memorial) pp. 9b, 12t, 16t, 16b, 17t, 18, 28t, 32–33 © Tomáš Fritta-Haas; 27b, 28b, 29t; 35t © Eva Odstrcilová, Tomáš Weisz, Pavel Weisz; pp. 39, 43t, 44b Terezín Memorial, Hermann Collection © Zuzana Dvoráková. © Photothèque CICR pp. 26b,

27t, 47, 50t, 51. USSHM p. 56t courtesy of Ivan Vojtech Fric. © Wallstein Verlag pp. 48, 49 by kind permission of Helga Weissová-Hošková. © Yad Vashem pp. 13t, 14 Collection of the Yad Vashem Art Museum, Jerusalem Gift of the Prague Committee for Documentation, Prague, courtesy of Ze' Ev Shek, Caesarea; p. 23 Jerusalem Gift of the Prague Committee for Documentation, Prague, courtesy of Alisa Shek, Caesarea; p. 29b Jerusalem Gift of the Prague Committee for Documentation, Prague, courtesy of Ze'Ev and Alisa Shek, Caesarea; p. 53b © Tomáš Fritta-Haas; p. 56b, 58, 59, 60t, 60b.

Every effort has been made to obtain permission from the relevant copyright holders and to ensure that all credits are correct. Any omissions are inadvertent and will be corrected in future editions if notification is given to the publisher in writing.

Maps pp. 8, 10 by Simon Roulstone